The World's Worst Scarecrow

'The World's Worst Scarecrow'
An original concept by Jenny Moore
© Jenny Moore

Illustrated by Valeria Abatzoglu

Published by MAVERICK ARTS PUBLISHING LTD
Studio 11, City Business Centre, 6 Brighton Road,
Horsham, West Sussex, RH13 5BB
© Maverick Arts Publishing Limited February 2021
+44 (0)1403 256941

A CIP catalogue record for this book is available at the British Library.

ISBN 978-1-84886-764-2

OXFORDSHIRE COUNTY COUNCIL	
3303634598	
Askews & Holts	19-May-2021
JF BEGINNER READER	

This book is rated as: Purple Band (Guided Reading)

The World's Worst Scarecrow

By Jenny Moore

Illustrated by Valeria Abatzoglu

"A-a-a-choo! Achoo!"

Poor Farmer Frank was in bed with a bad cold. Scarecrow Scarlet could hear him sneezing all the way from the cornfield.

"Oh dear," she said to a passing field mouse. "Who's going to milk the cows now? Who will feed the pigs and collect the eggs? And who's going to drive the tractor?"

"Aunt Anne's come to stay for a few days," squeaked the mouse. "I saw her getting out of the taxi last night. She'll be in charge of the farm until Farmer Frank's feeling better."

"That's kind of her," said Scarecrow Scarlet. "She sounds very nice."

"No, she's very cross and bossy," said the mouse. "I heard her telling Farmer Frank to turn off the radio and go back to sleep. Then she told the chickens to stop clucking and lay more eggs. She told the cows to make more milk and told the pigs to be less smelly."

Scarlet laughed. "It's a good job I'm just a scarecrow. At least she can't get cross with me."

But she was wrong...

Scarlet heard a cross, bossy cry. "Shoo! Get out of here!"

Scarlet saw a tall, thin lady marching up the hill. She was wearing a pair of Farmer Frank's muddy wellies and carrying a clipboard. She waved her clipboard at a pair of passing crows "Shoo!" she called again.

'That must be Aunt Anne,' thought Scarlet.

"What a disgrace," growled Anne. "Look at all these crows eating Frank's corn. He needs a better scarecrow." She prodded Scarlet in the tummy with her pen. "This tatty old one couldn't scare a fly!"

Scarlet's painted red cheeks turned even redder. It was true. Nobody was scared of her. No matter how hard she waved her broomstick arms and shook her scarecrow head, the crows kept on pecking.

Anne straightened Scarlet's hat and brushed the mud off her shirt. "I'd better keep my eye on this," she said. "If this old scarecrow can't scare the birds away, I'll have to find one that can."

Scarlet's straw-stuffed body shook.

'No,' she thought. 'Please don't get rid of me! I'll try harder. I'll scare those crows away. You'll see.'

It was no good. Scarlet just wasn't scary. She tried flapping her arms high in the air, but that didn't work. The cheeky crows flew under her arms and tickled her with their wings.

"Hee hee, stop it," cried Scarlet.

"Caw!" said the crows. "You really are ticklish." Then they went back to pecking Farmer Frank's corn.

Scarlet tried spinning round extra-fast in the wind, but that was no good. The crows rode on her shoulders like a fairground ride.

"Caw!" they cried. "This is fun! Faster! Faster!"

Soon there were more crows than ever, lining up for a turn.

15

Poor Scarlet. She tried telling them spooky stories to scare them. But that plan failed too. Her stories were too good. Even more crows flocked to the field to hear them.

"Caw! That was brilliant!" they said. "Tell us the one about the haunted barn again."

Scarlet sighed as the crows got back to their corn-pecking.

"Oh dear. Here comes Aunt Anne, looking crosser than ever."

Anne was furious when she saw the cornfield. "Right, that's it," she cried. "If those crows aren't gone by tomorrow, I'm getting a new scarecrow. A shiny Fright 4000 robot with laser eyes. That should scare those pesky birds."

Scarlet was awake all night trying to think of a plan. A new, super-scary plan. But she'd run out of ideas. The next morning, when the crows flew into the cornfield, they found her in tears.

"Caw, you look sad," they cried. "What's wrong?"

Scarlet told them about the robot scarecrow.

"Laser eyes? Caw! They sound terrible. We don't want a nasty Fright 4000 zapping us while we're trying to eat. We want you."

The oldest, wisest crow hopped onto Scarlet's shoulder.

"Don't worry," he said. "Your spooky stories have given me an idea." He flew off to the washing line and came back with a white bed sheet. "Here we are," he said, draping it over Scarlet's head. "Hold still," he added, dipping his beak in the mud and painting on scary eyes and a mouth. "Now turn around the other way so Aunt Anne can't see your face."

"Quick," cried another crow. "Here she comes."

"Everyone under the sheet," called the old crow. "And keep quiet until I give the signal."

It was very tickly with so many crows under the sheet. Scarlet couldn't help laughing – until she heard Aunt Anne stomping up the hill towards her.

"No crows today, I see," said Aunt Anne.

"Good. Make sure you keep it that way, or else."

"Caw!" called the old crow, giving the signal.

"CAWWWW!" screamed all the crows together, making a terrible ghostly noise. They flapped their wings underneath the sheet, making it rustle and move.

"Cawwww!" joined in Scarlet, spinning round to face Aunt Anne.

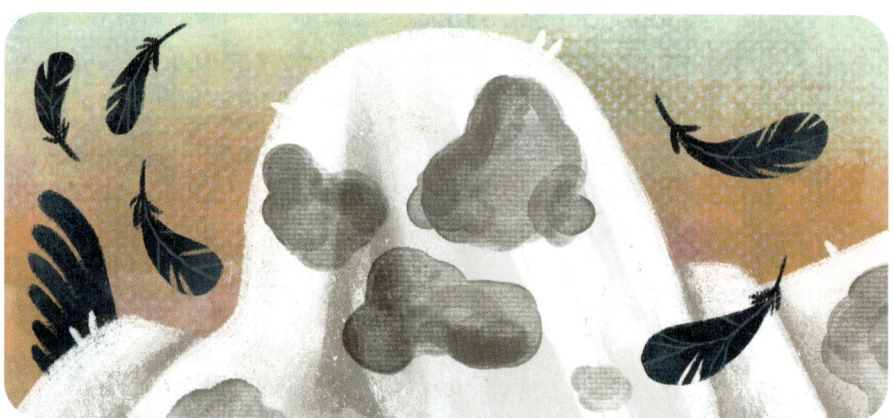

Aunt Anne took one look at the spooky mud face and screamed. She was still screaming as she ran back to the farmhouse to pack her bags.

"Achoo!"

Scarlet could hear Farmer Frank sneezing as he milked the cows the next morning. He was still sneezing as he fed the pigs and collected the eggs. But not as much as before.

It sounded like he was getting better.

"What happened to Aunt Anne?" Scarlet asked a passing field mouse.

"She left in a taxi last night," squeaked the mouse. "She said the farm was too scary and Farmer Frank would just have to manage on his own."

"How strange," said Scarlet, winking at her new crow friends.

"Caw," they agreed.

Quiz

1. Why was Farmer Frank in bed?
a) He was tired
b) He had a bad cold
c) He hurt his leg

2. Who came to do the farm work?
a) Aunt Mary
b) Uncle John
c) Aunt Anne

3. What is Scarlet supposed to do?
a) Plant seeds
b) Dance
c) Scare birds

4. What was the name of the robot scarecrow?
a) Fright 4000
b) Spooker 9000
c) Crow Scarer 500

5. What was the old crow's signal?
a) Hoot
b) Caw
c) Tweet

Book Bands for Guided Reading

The Institute of Education book banding system is a scale of colours that reflects the various levels of reading difficulty. The bands are assigned by taking into account the content, the language style, the layout and phonics. Word, phrase and sentence level work is also taken into consideration.

Maverick Early Readers are a bright, attractive range of books covering the pink to white bands. All of these books have been book banded for guided reading to the industry standard and edited by a leading educational consultant.

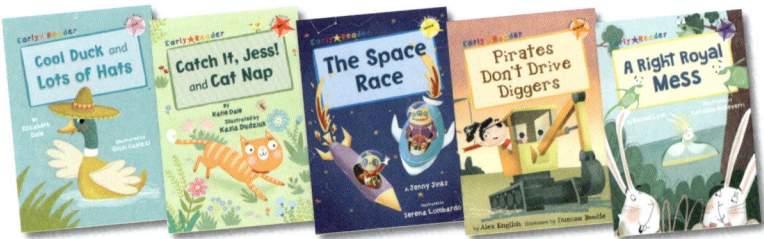

To view the whole Maverick Readers scheme, visit our website at www.maverickearlyreaders.com

Or scan the QR code above to view our scheme instantly!

Quiz Answers: 1b, 2c, 3c, 4a, 5b